D0984855

This Little Light

This Little Light

LESSONS IN LIVING
FROM SISTER THEA BOWMAN

Michael O'Neill McGrath

ORBIS BOOKS

Maryknoll, New York 10545

Founded in 1970, Orbis Books endeavors to publish works that enlighten the mind, nourish the spirit, and challenge the conscience. The publishing arm of the Maryknoll Fathers and Brothers, Orbis seeks to explore the global dimensions of the Christian faith and mission, to invite dialogue with diverse cultures and religious traditions, and to serve the cause of reconciliation and peace. The books published reflect the views of their authors and do not represent the official position of the Maryknoll Society. To learn more about Maryknoll and Orbis Books, please visit our website at www.maryknoll.org.

Library of Congress Cataloging-in-Publication Data

McGrath, Michael O'Neill.
  This little light : lessons in living from Sister Thea Bowman / Michael O'Neill McGrath.
    p. cm.
  ISBN-13: 978-1-57075-791-4 (cloth)
  1. Bowman, Thea. 2. Christian life—Catholic authors. I. Title.
  BX4705.B8113M34 2008
  271'.97302—dc22
                              2008012708

*"**B**e who you are and be that perfectly well."*

—*St. Francis DeSales*

*This book is lovingly and gratefully dedicated to
the Franciscan Sisters of Perpetual Adoration,
and to
Angelo Maraldo, osfs (1957-2008),
who makes beautiful music in Thea's heavenly choir.*

CONTENTS

ACKNOWLEDGMENTS

This project has been in the making since 1992, which is when I first began to share the story of Sr. Thea Bowman and the way she transformed my life as an artist and religious brother. I never dreamed at the outset that she would take me around the country to share these paintings at dozens and dozens of venues, beginning with the Office of Black Catholics in the Archdiocese of Philadelphia on a cold Super Bowl Sunday afternoon.

Each event had a wonderful gospel choir or soloists and so I feel supremely blessed to have met and worked with such fine church musicians who not only make joyful sounds of praise but who have enhanced my own creativity. So, first and foremost, I thank all of them, with special nods to Dan Johnson Wilmot at Viterbo University, Thea's amazingly talented colleague and friend who conducted the music at two events in LaCrosse and shared with me his own special memories of Thea; and to the musicians at World Library Publications who sponsored my first Thea events on the national convention scene.

I am most grateful to Sister Mary Ann Gschwind, FSPA, the sisters' archivist at the motherhouse in LaCrosse who was my first contact with the community; to Sr. Charlene Smith, FSPA, the community's advisor on all matters Thea; and Sr. Dorothy Kundinger, FSPA, Thea's friend, secretary, and companion who regaled me with stories in a truck stop diner in Mississippi. Each of them has blessed me with their generosity and hospitality—

and I am delighted they have become my friends. I would like to include here, as well, Mary Lou Jennings, founder of the Thea Bowman Black Catholic Education Foundation, which so uniquely carries on Thea's mission.

I want also to thank the members of my own Salesian family—my confreres in the Oblates of St. Francis DeSales who continually support and encourage me, especially Bro. Bob Drelich who keeps me somewhat sane; and the Sisters of the Visitation in Minneapolis who make Thea's spirit live on in their own special way.

Lastly, and by no means least, I thank Mike Leach, the gentleman and scholar who brought this project to Orbis Books, and the great Robert Ellsberg, my editor and inspiration. Their enthusiastic regard for Thea, and their belief in me, has made this book happen.

INTRODUCTION

Ilike to tell folks that I have a little black nun inside of me. She's my muse, my spiritual friend and inspiration. She's a patron saint who leads me and guides me when I call on her to lend me a hand. She's the late Sr. Thea Bowman (December 29, 1937- March 30, 1990) and though I never met her in the flesh I feel I know her well. In fact, I never even heard of her until after her death. But now that I mention it, death and dying are what brought us together in the first place. The paintings in this book tell that story. It's a life and death story of light.

"Each one teach one," she used to say, and so I try to do my bit. "When somebody does something for you, don't pay them back, pass it on to someone else." Well, that's what I am doing here, sharing these paintings and stories with you, these glimpses into her life which I have been so very blessed to receive. Maybe she will wheedle and prod you the same way she did for me. Maybe she will show you your very self as you have never seen yourself before, your wonders as well as your flaws, blessings and curses in one big happy family. Maybe she will show you a new face of Jesus, one that has been staring you in your clueless little eyeballs all along.

I don't know about you, but more often than not I really have to have things spelled out s-l-o-w-l-y and c-l-e-a-r-l-y, especially those pesky little mysteries in life like personal grace and eternal redemption. My sense is that God must be like one of those people who talks louder to foreigners thinking they will understand better. It's just like the great writer Flannery O'Connor once said, "To the hard of hearing you shout, for the almost blind you draw large and startling figures." Well, more often than not, that's the story of my life, and this is the best example I've got of a large and startling figure commissioned by God to get my attention. I think that God, weary and hoarse from trying, just gave up and sent the unforgettable, indefatigable Sr. Thea Bowman to teach me a thing or two. And now, hopefully, she can do the same for you.

She came to me personally much as she came to the world—as a shining light in a dark and wounded time. I was struggling with grief and the realization of being a thirty-five year old orphan, wondering what to do now that I was all grown up. I was bored with my work and intensely restless to see if I could be a "real" artist, you know, one who does it as a day job. I wanted to paint landscapes because they are nice and safe and pretty to look at. Or, more to the point, I really wanted to at last actually finish a painting or two because it was beginning to feel as if I'd never had that experience. Thea taught me that brooding perfectionism and wallowing in the darkness of self-pity are not the virtues of a full-fledged, practicing artist nor of a baptized Roman Catholic for that matter. Who knew? I thought I was supposed to be eternally melancholy and long-suffering as part of both deals. Throw being one hundred percent Irish in the mix and I didn't stand a chance.

The Latin root of the word redemption refers to being freed from slavery. I didn't realize how enslaved I was until Sr. Thea came along and said you don't HAVE to live as a slave of guilt, anxiety, and fear. You CAN have faith but be riddled with doubt. You CAN be happy with the life that has been given you, not that one over there that you only think you want. Everything you need for the journey is already inside, and best of all, you don't have to do it alone. That's what we are all here for, to guide each other along. Basically what she taught me is to love, to love the life which has been given me to live, to love myself whole and entire.

If you are in grief, let her show you how to live beyond the emptiness. If you are sick, let her show you how to live with the pain. If you are afraid and anxious, let her walk with you awhile and hold your hand. If you have lost sight of your beauty, let her hold up a mirror so you can see how beautiful you are. Can't you hear her say, "Maybe I need to see my beauty reflected in your eyes before I can realize I am a beautiful person. Until I have found the beauty in a person, I cannot help that person." So go ahead, help yourself. These were her reasons for living when she sang and danced among us; these are her reasons, still, in the heavenly choir.

The spiritual says, "Over my head I hear music in the air. There must be a God somewhere." So, sit back and relax, look at what's right in front of you with the eyes of your heart, listen real hard to the music within, know it must be God, and just keep on steppin'.

Chapter 1

Sometimes I feel Like A Motherless child

"*Lord, let me live until I die. If that prayer is answered,*
how long really doesn't matter."

"*Sometimes I feel like a motherless child,*
a long way from home."

Since this is a story about light I will begin there, on the sun-filled day in winter when Thea first introduced herself to me. In some ways, it was a perfectly typical Sunday afternoon with me flipping idly through some magazines on my father's coffee table, he napping peacefully just a few feet away. What wasn't so typical is that he was taking this nap in a hospital bed which had dominated the space of our living room for several months. He was dying of colon cancer and we all knew it. We were all bracing ourselves for it as much as we could, but having been through this with our mother just a few years before, we knew better than to think we could ever be fully prepared. Nonetheless, on that auspicious Sabbath day, the house was calm and quiet with clear, crisp sunshine pouring over us through the large picture window, he beneath his afghan, lightly snoring, myself on the couch, sadly serene.

It was not unlike the painting depicted here which I did shortly after my father died. It's based on a small pencil sketch I had done early one morning a few months before, right around Christmas. I was having my last cup of coffee before leaving for work and from my spot at the kitchen table, I could see straight into the living room where Dad's hospital bed was bathed in shadows and early morning light. So with a sketchbook at hand, I began to sketch my morning prayers. As I did, the sounds of the opera singer Kathleen Battle emanated from the television on top of the refrigerator, filling the air with liltingly beautiful Christmas music. It was one of those memorably ordinary present moments. You know the kind, when you have a heightened awareness of life, death, and the inscrutable mystery of God's presence over a cup of coffee. The painting's title, "Yonder Breaks a New and Glorious Morn," comes from the words I jotted down in the margins of my drawing as the singer sang her song. "The weary world rejoices…"

Anyhow, back to that first afternoon with Sr. Thea. One of the magazines I flipped through, US Catholic, had her last interview, entitled "On the Road to Glory," given shortly before she died. I'd never heard of her, never laid eyes on her beautiful smile or soulful eyes which peered out at me beneath an African turban in the small picture which accompanied the article. She utterly captivated me with her charm and the eloquence of her words. She shared brief recollections of the deep south in which she grew up and the wisdom she learned from the people who raised her. Her stories painted pictures in my mind of an entirely different world than I could have ever imagined in northeast Philly where I grew up, and where I sat that very afternoon.

A
Long,
Long,
Long Way
from home.

In sharing her own pains and fears so self-lessly, Sr. Thea exposed something universal about suffering which tickled me. She also reminded me that as people of faith we have within ourselves the capacity to let the light of grace shine through the cracks of our broken spirits. When she spoke of her own impending death it helped me to accept the reality of my father's upcoming death as something more than just bearable. It felt like a terrible but momentous beauty knocking at the door, a visitor to be welcomed with arms wide open. When I finished reading, I glanced over at my father tucked under his blankets, the weary traveler taking a Sunday snooze on his own glory road. That's how the whole experience felt, like the quiet and deep rejoicing of a weary world.

War was in the air then. The first war in Iraq, the one where scud missiles and Israeli kindergartners wearing gas masks filled the TV screen in the living room. Weirdly, the Gulf War became a bit of welcome distraction from war that cancer had waged on our homefront. The gentleness of Thea's words proved stronger than my battle fatigue and had a calming effect on many levels. I absorbed her words and prayed with them. Words about freedom from pain, freedom from want. Words about the light of Christ, which in the moment felt as warm and comforting as the wintry sunlight covering my father and me. Thea's words gave me a quiet kind of joy. And joy gave me hope, not hope that my father would get better, but hope that all would be well because we are all together traveling on that same road to glory, some of us just getting home a little sooner than the rest.

There were no bolts of lightning or thundering voices that afternoon, no startling moment of revelation. No, it was much subtler than that. In fact, it would be a safe bet that I just went to the kitchen for a snack when I finished because that's my usual response when momentous life change struggles to make itself known. As sacred mysteries go, it was a more subdued one like the Annunciation. Seed-planting time. It wasn't until a year and half after my father died in an unseasonably warm February that Thea reappeared, this time with more of the drama I have since come to associate with her.

It was a Thursday evening when I watched the video "Her Own Story" for the first of what would be literally dozens of times over the next years. I knew with every frame, every story and song that something profound and transformative was happening deep within. I couldn't sleep because of the images dancing in my head. The next morning I started to paint on sheets of heavy paper and didn't stop for almost two weeks, at which point there were nine new paintings scattered about the floor of my bedroom in a style very different from anything I'd done before. It was almost as if I didn't really paint them because they were such a huge departure from the overworked landscapes I'd labored on for years. I felt as if I were just a brush, stroking and pushing the colors of the Divine Painter, as my good friend Therese Martin once referred to God.

Buddhists say, "When the student is ready the teacher will appear." Well, this teacher didn't just appear, she possessed me. The images literally flowed out of me in no particular order without any kind of preliminary sketches. I just got myself out of the way, no easy task, and let the Spirit do her thing. I simply knew I was finished when I was finished and life hasn't been the same since.

Until that time I was painting those aforementioned unmemorable landscapes which never seemed to satisfy me. Maybe I have spatial depth issues, who knows? All I know is that Thea Bowman came along just in the nick of time to point out that the world doesn't need any more bad landscapes and, BREAKING NEWS: life is too damn short. She taught me so many other things as well: that whole new worlds of possibility wait patiently for us; that we're never too old to grow beyond those parts of our personalities that hold us back from being our best selves; that we can take a broken heart and a sin-sick soul, piece them together, and make them even better than before. I'd been an artist all my life, and even taught art for years, but now felt as if I were really seeing for the first time.

And, years later, I see that I didn't totally abandon my inclination towards landscape painting. You will see the colors of landscape throughout these nine paintings, but you won't see any landscapes. Thea's skin is the color of rich fertile soil, like a black Madonna. Her swirling lime green dresses are the hills and valleys, purple and gold are shadow and light. All the familiar elements were there but, like me, had been completely transformed.

I think the spiritual journey, the road to glory, is like that. We keep one foot in the familiar but let the other one fall God only knows where, hopefully following in the footsteps of the Spirit to our home far away. As Sr. Thea used to say, "It doesn't matter if you're scared, just keep on steppin'" And as that good old Christmas song says, "The weary world rejoices, for yonder breaks a new and glorious morn."

Chapter 2

Give Me That OLD Time Religion

"It takes a whole church to raise a child."

"It was good for my mother and my father.
It's good enough
for me."

The Holy Child Jesus mission was only a couple of years old in 1948 when four Franciscan Sisters of Perpetual Adoration came to town. They traded their familiar world of milk-white comforts in LaCrosse, Wisconsin, for the segregated cotton fields of Canton, Mississippi, in the deepest, darkest days of the Jim Crow South. Their lives were strangely defined by a color theme of black and white contrasts, beginning with the serge and starched linen of their habits and carrying over into the lives of the largely unchurched black sharecroppers whom they had come to serve and the unwelcoming white townsfolk who were most resentful of them for doing it.

No one group seemed to know what to fully make of the other, and in those early days, the sisters, who cut a very strange and exotic picture in their flowing habits, were treated in the same demeaning way as the black folks. When one of them registered to vote, the man at the desk, with all the southern hospitality he could cast aside, growled, "Why don't you n—— lovin' Catlicks go back north where you belong and mind your own business?" On the streets they were shunned, in stores they would have to wait at the end of the line and pay double for the picked-over produce. When the county finally granted permission for a Catholic school, they were told it must face away from the road with no sign and a high fence to conceal it. And so soon enough, these mightily determined women who would never dream of giving up (after all, God had brought them there) opened a one-room schoolhouse in a converted army barracks. (One moonlit night a year later, they tore down the fence themselves when construction began on a real school building.)

The first priests at Holy Child parish were Missionary Servants of the Most Blessed Trinity, who went there in 1946 at the request of Bishop Gerow to undertake work for the impoverished African-American community of the county. Several sisters from the same Trinitarian community came to Canton to assist them in the establishment of the parish. While they heroically performed the mammoth tasks of evangelization and social outreach, going door to door to invite the locals to church as well as setting up a clinic and kindergarten, they weren't a teaching order, and so couldn't properly staff a school. So, in 1948, the Franciscan Sisters of Perpetual Adoration arrived on the scene. Three of the women were teachers and the fourth was a nurse who visited homes and opened a small clinic for babies because of the high infant mortality rate in that part of the world. They registered 72 students that first year in grades one through six, none with a reading level higher than first grade.

Only one of the students was a Catholic. She was eleven year old Bertha Bowman, the only child of the town doctor, Theon, and his wife, Mary Esther, the daughter of a revered school-teacher. Driven by justice and compassion, Dr. Bowman had settled in Canton following medical school years before because no white doctors would treat black patients. The Bowmans were thrilled to enroll Bertha, who had only just become a Catholic the year before, at Holy Child Jesus and free her from the miseries of the public school system.

Bertha, a self-described nosey kid, used to hang out at the parish as it was being built. She had been searching for a church to call home, and shared many questions and conversations with the priests and sisters. Impressed by their joyful zeal and dedication, she soon decided to become a Catholic herself and was baptized in 1947 along with another little boy, raising the Catholic population to four out of four thousand African Americans in Canton. Intrigued as she was by the spiritual traditions of Roman Catholicism, she always maintained that it was really the witness of true Christianity as acted out by these joyful, hardworking sisters that most profoundly influenced her. And she passed the spirit on, influencing both of her parents to become Catholic many years later.

Bertha thrived in the Holy Child environ-

ment. She joined the children's choir and grew into a star pupil, immersing herself completely in the fine education she received from the Franciscan sisters. They were among the first white people she ever met, she said years later, who were kind and encouraging. They not only set her on a spiritual journey but offered her glimpses of a whole wide world beyond the cotton fields of Canton, a city not too far from Jackson. Eventually, Bertha Bowman came to believe that anything is possible when we let go of our fears, moving beyond them step by step, bit by bit, further away from our familiars into the exciting unknown territories of the Holy Spirit.

And so it came to pass that in 1953 at the age of sixteen, Bertha decided to leave home and become a Franciscan sister herself. Her father begged her not to go. Not only didn't he get this whole nun business, but he was terrified about his baby girl leaving the security of home for the cold, white North. The day she left home, he pleaded one last time, "Please don't go, they're not going to like you." To which she replied, "I'm going to make them love me." And off she went to the FSPA motherhouse in western Wisconsin on the banks of the Mississippi River, setting out to do just that.

On her profession day, Bertha became Sr. Thea, which means "of God." The name was cho-

sen in honor of her father, Theon. This teenager from the deep, deep South with gospel music in her bones, was as much a curiosity to the other sisters as they were to her. She once wrote home in a letter, "It's awful chilly up here and I'm not just talking about the weather."

As we see in this painting, Thea believed in those early days that all the things she was being taught would make her grow closer to God. After all, God was the One who called her there, so this must be what was required. Spiritual life was all about the externals. She sat upright, kept her habit perfectly creased in all the right places, and knelt real straight on the black and white tiles of Franciscan formation, just like all the white Wisconsin nuns they were forming her to be. But as we see in the subtle hints of this painting, Thea leaned in a different direction beneath the perfectly starched surface of convent life in the 1950s. She would always go against the grain, defiantly her own self, proud to be distinctly other, necessary traits for the confident and poised prophet she would eventually become.

Later in life, when Thea would sing "Give Me That Old Time Religion," she wasn't longing for the starched black and white formality of the church in those days, nor did she miss its stagnating emphasis on law and order. The old time religion of which she sang was about community, the church of her Southern black childhood, where people did for each other, raised each other's children, nursed each others' sick and elderly. A church where even the "characters" and outsiders could find a home. A church black and beautiful, ever ancient, ever new.

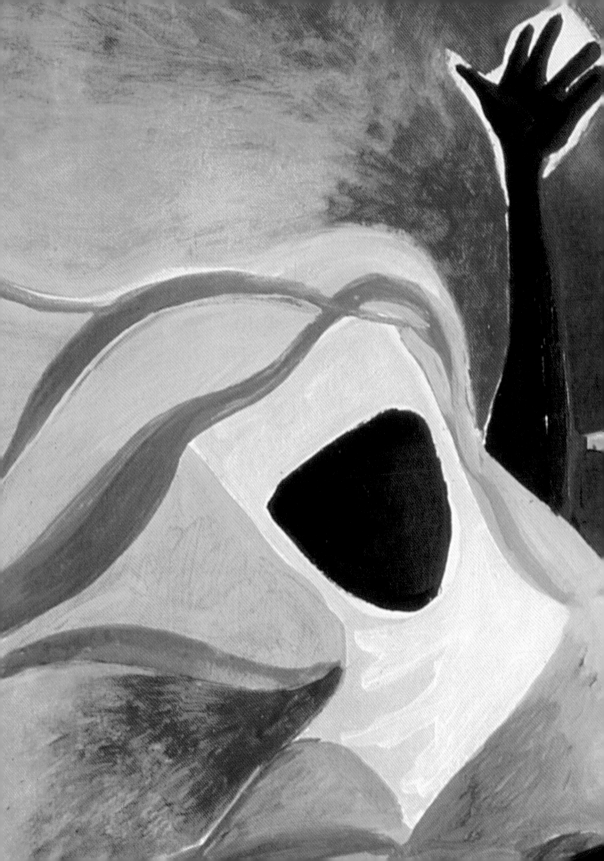

Chapter 3

This Little Light
OF MINE

*"Let your light shine. Each one teach one. Walk your talk.
You didn't get your light only to sit on it."*

"Jesus gave it to me, I'm gonna let it shine."

*This little light
of mine
I'm gonna let it
SHINE
letitshineletitshine
letitshine.*

It caused quite a stir when Sr. Thea returned to teach at Holy Child Jesus in 1961. Canton, Mississippi, was simply not ready for a black woman living in a house full of whites. Even servants didn't do that. When the community went shopping in town, Sr. Thea had to be driven by her parents and meet the other sisters there. If on occasion she did drive with the other nuns, she had to hunch down on the floor out of view. At one point Bishop Gerow, concerned for their safety, asked the sisters not to venture too far off the church property.

But despite the repressed air, or perhaps because of it, Thea began to soar, honing her skills as a teacher, speaker, and musician. To help raise money for the school, she made a record with her children's choir entitled "The Voice of Negro America," a collection of spirituals, the music of her slave ancestors. Thea's grandparents had taught her these songs as a little girl and now, in the dawning days of the civil rights marches, they were filling America's airwaves and becoming familiar to a whole new audience.

In 1966 Reverend Martin Luther King preached at Holy Child Jesus and was blessed by the pastor before leaving. Soon after, the freedom marchers found their way to Canton as well. Denied permission to hold a rally at the public school as they had been promised, over eight hundred

demonstrators slept on the gym floor at Holy Child Jesus. The sisters opened their convent to the ambulance workers and victims of tear gas and police brutality, all of it captured on national television. Over the next few days they fed sandwiches, cookies, and Kool-aid to one thousand people, and miraculously enough, they never ran out of "loaves and fishes." Despite their sleeplessness and exhaustion, they were deeply moved at meeting so many remarkable people, black and white, with such enormous dedication to the cause of justice.

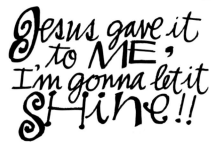

Most excitingly, the grassroots church was at the center of these historic changes. Bishop Gerow had sent word out to the parishes of the diocese: "Integrate or be excommunicated." The governor of Mississippi, Paul Johnson, even thanked the bishop for the calming presence of the Catholic church in the midst of the violent storm. Even though she was away at the motherhouse throughout those turbulent days of summer, Thea was swept up in the force of it all, developing a sense of community broader than the tightly knit village of her youth, newer than the Franciscan community of her young adulthood.

Of course, the students at Holy Child were caught up in the frenzy of it all and their response was often to lash out in angry protest. But Sr. Thea taught the children that nonviolence, as preached

by Dr. King, was the only true Christian response to the injustices surrounding them. Letting go of the sins of the past was the only way to move forward.

Just a week before my father died, my sister sat on the edge of his hospital bed telling him about her day at work when all of a sudden he began to cry. He said, "Suzanne, when I look back on my life I realize I worried too much about what other people thought of me. Other guys at work. Relatives. Neighbors. Don't do that to yourself," he went on, "don't ever keep your light under a bushel basket." He said his mother told him that from the time he was a young man, but he never listened. Down our family generations, this message of letting our lights shine was passed forward in a simple, death-bed conversation. It is a life-long reminder to me that Thea's recurring message was exactly the same: Each of us has a God-given light as well as a responsibility to let it shine. We must share the light in the best way we can and stop worrying about what other people think.

In "This Little Light of Mine," Sr. Thea moves forward in song and dance to the rhythms of a more universal sense of church, a higher call to seek justice and peace, a deeper love for the light within, freed forever from concern for what others think of her. "Remember who you are, and

Whose you are" became the motto of her transformed sense of self in the 1960s. She was on her way to becoming her true self, the one she was put on earth to be.

The black and white of her habit and floor have evolved into the brilliant green of new life and hope. She dances with Jesus, Eucharist and Light, Lord of the Dance and love of her life, breaking free forever from the narrow confines of the systemized segregation and bigotry that she knew as a girl in Mississippi. She breaks free as well from a relationship with God based on fear and uniformity. She walks in the light, sings in the light, dances in the light, preaches in the light. She has become more fully her true self, a shining light. This little light. Let it shine, let it shine.

Chapter 4

Everytime I Feel the SPIRIT

"I can't preach in the church. Women can't preach in the
Catholic church. But I can preach in the streets. I can preach in
the neighborhood. I can preach in the home. I can teach and
preach in the family. And it's preaching that's done in the home
that brings life and meaning to the Word your priest
proclaims in the pulpit."

"Everytime I feel the Spirit movin' in my heart I will pray."

every time
I feel the
Spirit
moving in my
Heart
I will pray.

In 1966, Thea once again left Canton and headed for the Catholic University of America in Washington, DC, to pursue graduate and doctoral studies. There was plenty of excitement and upheaval on college campuses in those days of student protests against the war in Vietnam, civil rights marches, and various liberation movements. In addition to the huge cultural changes sweeping the nation in 1968, the Catholic church experienced its own revolution as a result of Vatican II.

Thea's personal life was as radically changed by these developments as were the country's and the church's. Meeting and befriending other black Catholics and religious made her feel less of an anomaly not only in the Franciscans but in the church at large. She began to celebrate her heritage in new and dynamic ways, introducing traditional African-American music into the liturgy and giving lectures and performances on the history of black sacred music. She would explain the hidden symbols and codes that the slaves wove into the words in the spirituals, and then she would sing the songs.

No matter her topic or audience, music always came first. It was at the heart of her presentations because music is what she was most passionate about in her own heart. From the day she started music lessons and joined the children's

choir at Holy Child in Canton (her mother vol-
unteered as the pianist for the group) until the
day she died, singing and listening to beautiful
songs was her primary connection to God and to
God's children. And specifically, it was the spirituals that guided her to those prayerful places
deep within where she could feel one with the
Spirit and her ancestors. The spirituals were what
she heard pouring forth in graceful beauty from
the mouths of her grandparents and other folks
around town. In one way or another, every spiritual speaks of the human yearning for freedom
and the intense struggle involved in getting to that
place. Thea decided that her life-long mission
would be to pass these timeless and universal lessons to others of all races and backgrounds. She
was truly giving the gift given to her, and in the
giving she was set free.

Thea, who could barely read when she
started fifth grade at Holy Child Jesus, received a
Masters degree in English in 1969 and earned a
PhD in English Language, Literature, and Linguis-
tics in 1972. In between, she taught the first-ever
class on black literature at Catholic University, and
to feed her passions for Shakespeare and the writ-
ings of St. Thomas More she studied for a summer
at Oxford University in England.

Once she received her doctorate, Thea returned to her motherhouse in LaCrosse where she taught English at Viterbo College and became heavily involved in public speaking, drama, and music. She formed a choir called the "Jubilee Singers" who performed spirituals and gospel music. In addition, every summer for ten years, Thea delivered scholarly papers on her favorite writer, William Faulkner, at the University of Mississippi alongside such writers as Toni Morrison and William Styron.

Sr. Thea was a born teacher who truly flourished in the academic environment. When teaching southern literature at Viterbo, she took students on bus trips to the south, explaining that unless they saw the land, tasted the food, and heard the music, they wouldn't truly understand what southern literature was all about. Sometimes, she would walk into class and sing a spiritual to get the class going. "I gotta get you kids motivated," she'd explain, "especially you white kids." When her song was finished, class began.

One of her proudest life achievements came in 1980 when Thea helped to found the Black Catholic Studies Institute at Xavier University in New Orleans. She remained on the faculty for the rest of the decade, teaching courses on liturgy, intercultural awareness, and African-American spirituality.

ALL around ME looked SO SHINE, ASKeD MY LORD if all WAS MINE

The winds of change and renewal wash over Thea in this painting. An African dress and scarf, still green as in the previous painting, has replaced the religious habit. This painting is about those come-home-to-Jesus times in our lives when we must break with our past and move forward, perhaps a little fearfully, into unknown futures. We do so in faith, trusting that the same God who watched over us yesterday will still be there tomorrow, and every day. Only in our Spirit-filled moments can we rest comfortably in the present moment, free of those painful memories and bitter resentments that keep us mired in the past, as well as the worries and anxieties that tie us to an unknown future.

Thea taught that we must learn to welcome our pains and struggles as teachers who can lead us and guide us to the freedom that comes from being our true selves, children of the light. For Christians this only makes sense in the context of Jesus' own suffering. May the wind of the Spirit purify us and set our dancing feet on a path toward the Light.

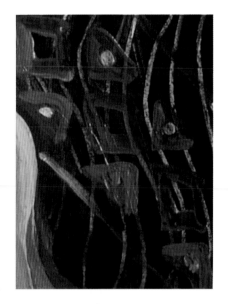

jordan river, chilly & cold, chills the body but not the soul.

Chapter 5

I'll Be Singing up there

"St. Francis said that all his followers needed were to be minstrels and troubadours going about the countryside, teaching the good news, singing and praising. Somebody like me was made to be a minstrel and troubadour."

"If you miss me singing down here,
Come on up to bright glory, I'll be singing up there."

When the slaves sang this song, with its images of "comin' on up to bright glory" and "missing me down there," they were really singing about living in freedom up North, not some far distant heaven as the words might first suggest. Freedom is a bright glory and the only way to get there is together. Thea the Franciscan troubadour loved to perform these songs and Thea the scholar loved to de-code them, explaining the hidden meanings of the symbols. The spirituals weren't just heartwarming songs that reminded her of home and her grandparents who taught them to her. For Thea, they were modern American compositions equal in importance to the psalms and lamentations of the Hebrew scriptures. They were great literature to be sure, but more importantly, they were the main source of her prayer and meditation. They were the wisdom literature of her ancestors with valuable lessons for all people no matter their race or background.

From the beginning of her life as a Franciscan sister, Thea was known as a gatherer of God's minority children. She loved reaching out to the outsiders in her midst and introducing them to each other. When she converted to Catholicism at the age of ten, she was essentially the only Catholic among the blacks and the only black among the Catholics. She loved the liturgy and the spirituality of Catholi-

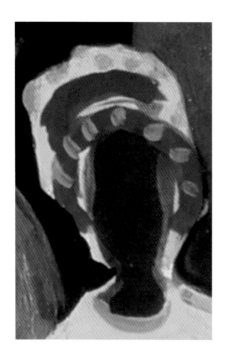

cism but she was more inspired by the religious sisters who were the ultimate outsiders among their fellow whites in town. She was profoundly moved by their cheerfulness in the midst of constant opposition as well as their unwillingness to tolerate racism in any way. They taught love not hatred.

When she first moved to LaCrosse, Wisconsin, in 1954, it was two years before she met another African American, but quickly forged a friendship to make up for lost time. Thea also maintained a special affection for the Native Americans who lived on a reservation in the diocese. It was her great gift to just be herself around others, no matter the group's race, gender, age, or religious background. She empowered others through this gift, encouraging them to be themselves as well.

In 1978, Thea returned to Canton for good. Wanting to be present to her elderly parents, she moved back into her family home. Once there, Bishop Brunini asked her to start an Office of Intercultural Awareness for the diocese of Jackson, which she did, characteristically enough, with nothing but enthusiasm and imagination. Over the course of the next decade, Thea progressed from visiting schools throughout Mississippi where she gave presentations on intercultural matters to becoming a renowned figure in great demand on the national Catholic speaking circuit, giving over one

hundred presentations a year, singing, dancing, praying her way into people's hearts around this country and Africa.

No matter the topic or theme, no matter the audience or convention, her message was always the same: we need to cherish our own unique giftedness before we can appreciate the gifts of another. We need to share the wealth of what we've been given, not just materially, but spiritually as well. Thea rejoiced in the memory of the wisdom figures who filled her world as a child and who taught her lessons for life. "The elders made a deliberate effort to teach me about life, about love, about happiness and joy, about how to deal with insecurity and convince me I was special." Her ministry as an adult was to share that deep-down joy that comes from being a child of God, an "old folks' child," as she put it.

Because her presentations always began with a resounding, "Can you hear me, Church?," or "Are you with me, Church?," Thea let each person in her audience know immediately that they were not alone in their fears and concerns. But then, in her own colorful and inimitable way, Sr. Thea encouraged them to move beyond the comfort zones of the familiar. She'd say, "If every day I commit myself to do what I can do, then I can help to change the world." She

I'LL BE Singing UP THERE, OH! COME ON UP to Bright Glory, I'LL BE Singing UP there.

If You Miss Me Singing Down Here, Oh, Come On Up to bright Glory, You'll find Me Singing up there.

Singing praying WALKING SHOUTing

made changing the world and making it a better place seem doable and ordinary. And coming from her, it was a much less daunting task because she always pointed out that as church we are all in this together: "You walk together and you won't get weary. You might get tired, but you won't get weary."

Like any artist of faith, Thea believed that beauty could save the world, that all people, especially God's poorest and most neglected, would be profoundly touched by the beauty of poetry and song. It is what troubadours do. It is what the church has done since its earliest days when paintings were scrawled on catacomb walls. So, when Thea got the crowds on their feet, moving, swaying, leading them in song, she wasn't merely entertaining them, she was transforming them, moving their hearts and filling their tired, restless spirits with the love of God. She gave them new ways of locating beauty in the world, deeper and broader than the images of beauty offered by society. Thea led them from the surface of the familiar to locate beauty deep within.

I grew up in an environment where everyone I knew was white and Catholic except for one Lutheran girl down the street. And that was my brush with the exotic. That ended in my high school years when I took art lessons at the Moore College of Art in downtown Philly where for the first time I met black kids, Puerto Rican kids, and Jewish kids. Every Saturday we were creating together, laughing and having a good time, expanding our horizons forever through art. I learned how to literally see the world with new eyes and thus discover beauty in places I'd never been.

This painting was inspired by what I most loved about Thea the first time I saw that video of her life: the unique way she bridged art and faith. All the old forms of music, art, and poetry, all of which have always been the life blood of the church, came alive in new and exciting ways. She showed how these ancient prayer forms could be relevant to us today, in the modern American church. And, more importantly, how each of us could be a part of it.

If we could sing each others' songs, as Thea the great troubadour would say, we could walk through each others' neighborhoods without fear. Art doesn't fear the other, it celebrates otherness. When we throw religious faith in the mix, with its celebration of poetic beauty and ancestral wisdom, we see that we are all just works in progress, linked together like the beads of a rosary, each with a place at the table and helping each other to get there. We are empowered. We are ennobled. We are sanctified. We make the world and the church a place of bright glory.

Chapter 6

Precious Lord, take my Hand

"When I hurt I like to sing some of the old songs. I find that prayer and song can take me beyond the pain."

"I am tired. I am weak. I am worn . . .
Through the storm, through the night, lead me on to the light,
take my hand, precious Lord, lead me home."

1984 presented itself as a year of great change and challenge for Thea. In March, at the age of forty-seven, she was diagnosed with breast cancer. Told she had three months to three years to live, Thea underwent a radical mastectomy and began chemo and radiation treatments. Later in the year both of her parents died, her mother in November and her father in December. Ushered into a new phase of life, one she hadn't exactly asked for, Thea gradually learned to welcome the suffering as a way to minister to others, a new revelation of God's compassionate and abiding presence which, like all gifts from God, was given her to share. "I'm gonna live 'til I die," became her credo as she lived more fully into each day, accepting each present moment as gift and grace.

Thea continued her grueling schedule of travel and speaking engagements without complaint. She still opened each talk in the same way: gliding across the stage in her flowing African dress she would step up to the microphone and ask, "Are you with me, Church?" Once the hooting and cheering subsided, she'd say, "We're all in this together, black, white, male, female, clergy, lay—and even bald!" as she'd whip off the turban wrapping her head. That was Thea's way, to reveal the truth of her condition right at the start so the audience could hear her message without the distraction of wondering if she was going to make it through. She refused to show any discomfort she may have been feeling, determined to preach and testify for as long as was humanly possible. And to do so with nothing but joy.

Where did this amazing stamina come from? Thea drew on the energy of the "ol' folks' child," the inner child of her spirit who remained enamored of the elders, observing them, listening to their song, learning from them their unique ways of locating inner peace in the midst of tribulation. They would hum their prayers for strength and moan their prayers for comfort from pain. Music was the heart and center of Thea's young world as well as her ministry as an adult, and it was what sustained her in times of suffering and need. When she sang the words of the spirituals, she became the living embodiment of God's abiding love. When she moaned or hummed without words, she could more readily enter into Jesus' passion. Music helped her come to terms with her suffering as nothing else could.

Continuing to work with people, especially children, also helped to take her mind off her pain. She said that suffering forced her to clarify her relationships and take stock of what was really important in life. She could speak from experience to children whose families were touched by breast

Precious Lord, take my hand, lead me on, let me stand,

I am tired. I am weak. I am worn.

Through the storm, through the night, Lead me on to the light, take my HAND, precious Lord, Lead me HOME.

cancer and help to calm their fears. She appeared in an interview by Mike Wallace on "Sixty Minutes" and clearly touched him to the core with her humor and humility.

After a period of remission, the cancer returned in 1988, invading her ribs and shoulders. When it reached her hips, she cut her engagements in half and began to work from a wheelchair. Before she took the stage to begin her talks, announcements would be made asking the crowds not to touch or hug her because even the slightest touch caused her great pain. In their excitement at the end of the talks, people sometimes ignored this and proceeded to touch her anyway. Asked once how she handled it, Thea replied, "In all His suffering, Jesus never said a mumbling word, so who am I?"

In this scene, Thea the storyteller tells a tale of salvation to the darkness. That is exactly why the spirituals were composed in the first place. Her ancestral songs used images and figures from the Old Testament to make parallels with their own yearnings to be freed from slavery. In the process they took pain and transformed it into something life-giving. They took ugliness and created beauty in its place.

Just as God led the Israelites to the Promised

Land with a pillar of fire in the night, Thea reminds us that the brilliant light of Christ is higher, deeper, and wider than the very formidable power of despair. The ol' folks' child has grown into the wisest and most loving of old folks herself, generously sharing her own beautiful story, sowing seeds of hope in a world in such desperate need if it. She points with dignity to the powerful source of all light, in Whose light we see light.

Chapter 7

Wade in the Water

Rise Up, Shepherd, and Follow

"I bring a spirituality that is communal, that tries to walk and talk and work and pray and play together, even with the bishops."

"God's gonna trouble the water."

There was plenty in Thea's story to make her a bitter and angry woman. When she was just five, she was spit on by a white woman for picking a flower from a tree in the woman's front yard. The Catholic church which she joined in 1947 had the same "colored only" pews as the other Christian denominations throughout the South, with the added feature of a "colored" area in the back for the reception of Holy Communion, far from the altar rail where whites received. (Since Holy Child Jesus was founded as a black parish, it didn't have these restrictions.) The day she left home for the convent in 1953, she traveled by train with several sisters. Told she had to go in the last car for the "colored," the outraged nuns cajoled and bargained until permission was granted for her to travel with them. After the voting rights act had been passed, she had to be flanked by federal marshals when she registered to vote at the county court house. But despite it all, bitterness and anger were never an option for Sr. Thea Bowman.

Thea learned early on from her parents how self-defeating it is to harbor grudges and resentments. She rose above the anger which could have consumed her, choosing instead a spirit of optimism and acceptance. She kept her eyes on the prize, Jesus, and focused her love on a church which was diverse in its universality, universal in

WADE in the
Water,
CHILDren,
GOD'S GONNA
trouble
the Water.

LOOK OVER
YONDER,
WHAT DO I See?
the Holy Ghost
a COMING on
Me

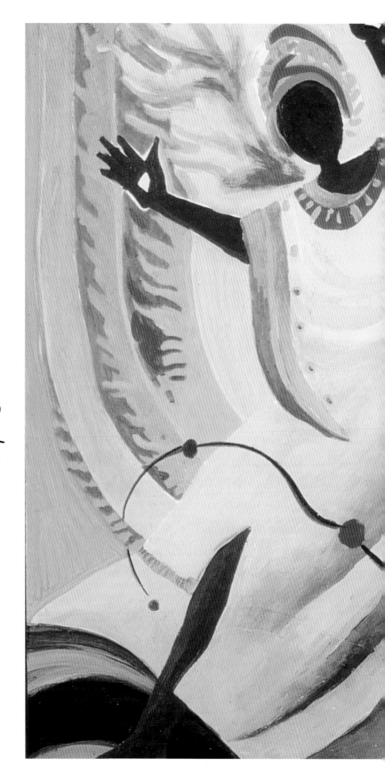

its diversity. She recognized, even celebrated, that this ever ancient, ever new church is much bigger than the very human weaknesses and failings of its leadership. After all, the same church whose hierarchy and monasteries owned slaves in the nineteenth century is the same church whose priests and religious built schools and clinics for the desperately poor blacks of the south. The same American church whose hierarchy never uttered a word against the immorality of slavery (and, in fact, some bishops openly condoned the practice using scripture as justification), nor spoke as a body against racism until the late 1950s (though the Vatican had done so over the ages), is the same church which spiritually and morally formed the bishops, priests, and religious who walked in the front lines of freedom marches and protests.

This very human church was, and is still, in desperate need of Thea Bowman. Her passionate love for outsiders and her need to gather them together sprang from the fact of her own marginalization growing up a black Catholic in Mississippi. What better authority than Sr. Thea Bowman to travel the country speaking on matters of discrimination in our church and nation? Who better than Sr. Thea Bowman to consult with the black bishops of the United States when they were drafting a pastoral letter called "What We Have Seen and Heard" on the evangelization of blacks in the Catholic church? What prominent American Catholic could speak with as much first-hand experience about the healing power of forgiveness and the need for institutional acknowledgement of the gifts of its African-American children? Who, then, was a better choice than Sr. Thea Bowman to address the United States Conference of Catholic Bishops on the topic "To Be Black and Catholic" at their annual meeting in 1989 at Seton Hall, New Jersey?

She began with the most perfect song. "Sometimes I Feel Like a Motherless Child," probably the most beloved of all spirituals, is about the abandonment of children under the brutal system of slavery. Of all the horrors that were endemic to that system, the worst was the abuse of children being torn from their mothers' sides, leaving them with lifelong feelings of longing and lonely despair.

The fact that such a beautiful hymn could be born from such unspeakable human pain cuts to the very heart of the message Thea delivered to the leaders of her mother, the church, on that summer day of June 17, 1989. Through the profoundly moving text of the spiritual and the broken quality of her weakened voice, Thea broke open the gospel for the bishops in the most startling and memorable way she could.

The haunting refrain expresses the intense

loneliness of being a "long way from home," so Thea's first spoken words flowed from there. "Can you hear me, Church? Jesus told me the church is my home, and Jesus told me that heaven is my home and I have here no lasting city. Cardinals, archbishops, bishops: My brothers, please help me to get home."

Courageous, prophetic, and prayerful, Thea gently but firmly reminded the bishops that the best preaching doesn't necessarily happen in the Sunday pulpit, but rather in the home and homeless shelter, in the celebration not only of the Eucharist, but in family, education, and culture—all of the places from which we come to our faith. She proclaimed a church in which all people can share the uniqueness of their gifts.

Thea spoke to them about inclusion of all God's children at the table, and about empowerment not power. "Go into a room and look around," she told them, "and see who's missing and call them in." Her urgent message to them was that we as church must listen to the voices of the poor and uneducated and that it is their role as leaders and teachers to show us the way.

Despite the rigors of difficult travel in getting there, and the lack of handicapped accessibility for her wheelchair to get on stage, Thea gave the speech of her life. She dazzled and captivated the bishops, never showing the slightest indication of the incredible pain and discomfort she was feeling. In the course of her profoundly beautiful remarks, she made the bishops laugh and cry and cajoled them onto their feet as she led them in a rousing chorus of "We Shall Overcome," their arms crossed and hands locked together in the gesture of freedom marchers back in the day. At the end of her speech, the bishops presented her with a dozen roses which she held in the air and proclaimed, "I accept these roses in memory of all the women who have nurtured you into the episcopacy." And they cheered some more.

There are great lessons to be learned from this shining episode in Thea's life, her last great sermon. By the time she had reached that magical day, she had broken entirely through the boundaries of concern for what others thought of her. It was enough for her to know, in genuine humility, that she was who she was; that a "what you see is what you get" attitude is the pathway to genuine holiness; that she couldn't possibly hold back the gift of herself from anyone at all, especially a roomful of bishops who needed to receive that precious gift; that each of us does God's will merely by loving the uniqueness of our gifts and stories and sharing them freely with others without caring what they think of us; that ours is an extravagant

God whose love, grace, and forgiveness never stop. It is we who block the blessings, we who choose fear over love time and again.

In this painting we see Sr. Thea Bowman handing over her timely and prophetic message to a group of startled and hesitant shepherds. Walking on water, she is enflamed with passion as she explains that God's children require more than just tolerance as members of the church. We each have a voice and must be provided the means to share the gift of who we are and Whose we are.

Even though she preached from a wheelchair that unforgettable summer day, in this painting Thea wades in the water as she hands over her precious message of hope, faith, and love. Her words and actions demonstrated to these symbols of power that fullness of life in Jesus is really about each of us in the church being empowered to share the unique discipleship that is ours. It is what we bring to the table of plenty where there should be room for all. "Jesus gave it to me, I'm gonna let it shine."

Chapter 8

Deep River

"I grew up with people who believed you could serve the Lord from a sickbed or a deathbed."

"Deep river, my home is over Jordan.
Deep river, I want to cross over into campground."

In the last year of her life, Sr. Thea was bestowed awards and honors from groups and universities throughout the United States, including eleven honorary doctorate degrees. President Ronald Reagan recognized her in an honorary letter as did the governors of several states. "Sr. Thea Bowman Day" was declared twice in Canton, and Baton Rouge made her the honorary mayor. Dozens and dozens of certificates, ribbons, and plaques began to fill the tiny home on Hill Street where she had been raised.

Sr. Thea was honored and grateful for all the fuss, but mostly she wanted to be remembered for her smile. She said that whenever other people leave our company, they should leave feeling better about themselves. For her, every encounter was a ministry of joy. Even death. People who came to visit Thea in her last days left her presence feeling more buoyant and grateful because of her graciousness and killer smile.

Dan Johnson Wilmot is the man who took over Thea's job as choir director of the Jubilee Singers when she left Viterbo and returned home to Canton in 1978. Of all her jobs and functions there, that was the hardest one for her to give up, but she was glad to mentor Dan into the position. Over the years they stayed in close contact and became very good friends, even to the point of referring to each other as brother and sister. Several weeks before she died, Dan gave her a most unique and wonderful gift: he brought the college choir to her tiny family home in Mississippi to perform for her one last time.

Forty students, standing shoulder to shoulder, crammed themselves into the tiny living room. Thea, whose bedroom was the adjoining room, refused to listen to this heavenly concert through the door and insisted on being in the living room with the students. Because of her extreme frailty, it took a half hour just to move her from one room to the next and get her comfortably situated. In the course of a very emotional goodbye with lots of tears, Dan casually mentioned to Thea that they would all be stopping at McDonald's for lunch on their way out of town before heading north to Wisconsin.

Dan was seated near a window at McDonald's eating his lunch when he noticed a car pulling into the parking lot. The rear window rolled down and there sat Thea. Dan motioned to the choir and the forty students left their tables, surrounded the car, and right there in the Canton McDonald's parking lot, sang "Deep River," Thea's favorite spiritual, a hauntingly beautiful hymn about death and crossing the River Jordan. No words were exchanged. She simply waved goodbye, rolled up the window

Deep River, my home is over Jordan; deep river, Lord, I want to cross over into campground.

and was driven home. Several weeks later, in accord with Thea's very detailed plans, Dan sang "Deep River" at her funeral.

In the beautiful tribute which accompanies the Laetare Medal, the highest award bestowed by Notre Dame University, and given posthumously to Sr. Thea Bowman, it says, "…it seems appropriate today for us to marvel at the manner in which grace withstands evil, like the flower which splits rock by growing. We are all descendants of sin and history, descendants of slavers and slaves, who have both wielded power and felt its scourge. But even the most monstrous monuments of human pride are no match for a flower named Thea with deep roots in African forests, Assisi hills, and the Mississippi Delta."

Sr. Thea Bowman died at the age of fifty-two in the early morning of Friday, March 30, 1990 at her family home in Canton. She was surrounded by family and friends, including several sisters from her community. Sister Dorothy, her best friend, said the rosebush in the backyard came to full bloom that very morning.

This painting is the simplest of any in the series. I knew I would have to paint a scene of her death, but I put off painting it until the very end because I wanted to work up to the pure simplicity of it all. More often than not, the things that appear the most effortless on the surface are the very things born of the most effort.

Thea lived her life that way. Her eloquent words, audacious humor, inspired songs, and graceful movements across stages and sanctuaries throughout the country, to countless throngs of people, were not only often shared in the midst of great physical pain and exhaustion, but had their very origin in her life-long witness of racism, sorrow, and strife. "It doesn't matter if you're scared, just keep on steppin'."

Chapter 9

I'll fly Away

"Tell them what Sojourner Truth said:
'I'm not going to die. I'm going home like a shooting star.'"

"When the shadows of this life have grown, I'll fly away;
like a bird from prison bars has flown, I'll fly away."

When she was just a girl, Thea's grandfather would share with her his stories and recollections of life as a slave. He always said that the worst kind of slavery isn't when you have chains around your ankles, but when you have chains around your heart. He said all people, no matter their color, have those chains. Thea heard this message and decided that when she grew up, she wanted to be someone who would help others to break the chains that surround their hearts. The best way, the most authentic way for her to do that was through song and worship. Through the one-of-a-kind work of art that she had created of her life, Thea empowered others to see their own lives as if for the first time and replace their hearts of stone with hearts of flesh. In her celebration of life, she taught others how to truly live with passion and gusto. "I'm gonna live 'til I die" is a motto for all folks, not just the terminally ill.

Slaves were often forced by their masters to sing spirituals while they were working so that they couldn't have conversations. What the masters didn't realize when they heard the music, was that the slaves were actually praying with and for each other through coded messages. One of the underlying meaning of "Swing Low, Sweet Chariot," for example, may be explained by the wagons that had hidden compartments on the bottom for sneaking slaves across the Mason-Dixon line. The texts of these songs brought Moses and the Promised Land as well as Jesus in His passion to new and meaningful life from the dusty pages of history and scripture.

And quilts were more than mere blankets. Slaves were forbidden to have any kind of grave marker, so when slaves died or moved away forever, never to be heard from again, a new block was added to the family quilt as a symbol of their memory. In this way, quilts became a sort of family tree and a way to keep memories alive of those who had passed. Often the designs were of African origin, passed down from generation to generation.

Thea loved the stories of her ancestors because of the wealth of wisdom and spiritual encouragement that could be found there. They provided her with lessons in living as well as dying. She grew up an ol' folks' child who learned that death is just a part of life, that we mustn't live our lives in fear of dying. Why fear going home? Why fear Jesus? Why fear freedom?

In the painting "I'll Fly Away" Thea rises from her deathbed and heads home. She has broken through all the chains of this world, free at last. She has crossed the river Jordan, free at last. She

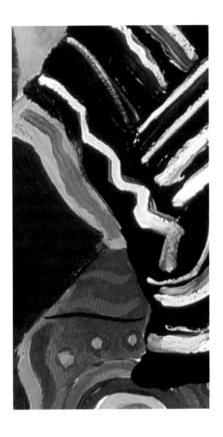

walks and sings in campground, free at last. She gazes at the face of Jesus with all the ancestors and saints who were her leaders and guides while she walked among us, free at last. She stands proud and tall, an icon of saintly courage and holy joy for the generations to come, free at last, free at last, free at last.

Chapter 10

We Shall Overcome

"Maybe I'm not called to make big changes in the world, but if I have somehow helped or encouraged somebody along the journey then I've done what I'm called to do."

"Deep in my heart, I do believe that we shall overcome someday."

Once, as I was wrapping up a school presentation on Sr. Thea's life, a second grader put up his hand and asked me why Sr. Thea was all of a sudden so big in this painting when she had been so skinny in all the others. On the spot, all I could think to reply was that she'd been eating at the heavenly banquet. I think it seemed to please him. I know it worked for me.

When Fr. Andrew Lawrence opened the parish mission of Holy Child Jesus with several confreres in 1946, he had no way of knowing what brilliant light and beauty would emerge as a direct result of his courage and vision. Because no property owners would sell land to the diocese for a Catholic parish, let alone one that would be ministering to blacks, he ended up with some neglected, mosquito-ridden acreage nicknamed "frog hollow" and set up two army barracks as church and clinic. Guided only by faith and tenacity, and helped by his confreres and associates in community, he followed his dream of bringing Christian love and hope to this third-world corner of the country. His guiding principle came from Fr. Thomas Judge, the founder of his religious community, the Missionary Servants of the Blessed Trinity: "Save the child and you save all."

He overcame.

When four Franciscan Sisters of Perpetual Adoration traveled south from Wisconsin to open a school on a neglected piece of swampland surrounded by cotton fields, they were "responding to an urgent need of the mid-twentieth century church." They agreed to a charity contract, which meant they would take no salary until one could be provided, however long that would be. So, three teachers and a nurse worked tirelessly against all odds to teach the children, tend to the sick, and nurture the gifts of these desperately poor, un-churched sharecroppers. They agreed as a community to boycott any store which would not serve black customers. They opened a school, a clinic, a thrift shop, and gave music lessons to one very special little girl.

They overcame.

When young Bertha Bowman left her home in the Mississippi delta, her "little cotton patch," as she called it, in the deep South and headed north to Wisconsin, she didn't abandon her family and elderly neighbors, her stories and traditions, her music. She carried them with her in her heart on that long train ride. She gradually learned to walk with confidence and poise in new worlds of glory with wider horizons. She didn't neglect one segment of her life for the sake of the other. She learned to bridge them, expanding not only her own vision, but the hopes and dreams of all who came into contact with her. She basked in diversity, celebrated variety, and unearthed the hidden gifts of everyone she met.

She overcame.

The series ends where it began, with Thea praying. She's once again dressed in black and white, as she was in the first painting, only the more formal and austere shapes of the old days have reconfigured themselves into lively patterns from Africa. I think that beneath all the changes we endure in life and the losses we suffer, through all the joys and flashes of success, we basically remain the same child longing to get home in the arms of our mothers. Only different. Clothed in the wisdom of our ancestors and saints, we learn to forgive. We forget. We say, " Thank you, God" and we just keep on steppin'.

We overcome.

WE SHALL
Overcome
WE'LL WALK
HAND IN HAND
WE SHALL
ALL HAVE
peace
WE Are Not
AFRAID
GOD IS ON
Our Side.

Chapter 11

The Windsock
VISITATION

"I know that God is using me beyond my comprehension. God has given me the grace to see some of the seeds I've sown bear good fruit, and I am so grateful."

"Everywhere I go, I'm gonna let it shine."

They are called the nuns in the 'hood, but their official title is the Sisters of the Visitation of Holy Mary. They live in a monastery on the north side of Minneapolis. I first met them when they hosted an open-house during a spirituality conference and a bunch of us drove over from St. Paul to check the place out. Trust me, it is not your grandmother's monastery.

A brief history: In 1989, four sisters decided to leave the cozy comforts of the academies for refined young ladies where they had spent their entire monastic lives and open a monastery in the midst of the poor. Most people thought they were crazy to abandon their familiar lifestyles and ministry, but they were determined to honor the call of the wild and forge a new way of living out their centuries-old Salesian spirituality. They felt that full immersion into life amid God's poorest and neediest was precisely what their founders, Sts. Francis DeSales and Jane DeChantal, had in mind in 1610 when the order was founded in Annecy, France.

Gradually, a custom evolved in the Minneapolis community in which a windsock is hung outside the house every other day as a sign to the children in the neighborhood that the monastery is open for after-school care and playtime. They read, they ride bikes, they learn manners, and have birthday parties. They go to plays and circuses and

this is the
PLACe OF
OUr DELight
and rest,
St. Jane de Chantal

summer camp, concluding every visit with a snack and prayer around a peace pole in the backyard. No matter what else is going on in their lives, these very blessed kids learn that God is love and that they are children of God.

How Thea-esque, I remember thinking as their story unfolded on that first visit to take their spirituality, something so old, so tried and true, and refashion it into something relevant to our world today. Their mission is to share the priceless gift of contemplation in a poverty-stricken atmosphere of distraction, noise, and chaos; or as they put it, to be a gentle presence in a violent world. In that, they are absolutely no different from what monasteries have been since the first days of monasteries in the desert: oases of prayer and gentle reminders that God whispers life and grace into the corners of the most unexpected places.

I was smitten. Suddenly I'd re-discovered what church can and should mean, a church which Thea had shown me is possible if hard to find. Women and men, black and white (and every color in between), American-born and immigrant, young and old, religious and lay, poor and comfortable, gay and straight, addicted and sober, all were welcomed at the door, all were invited to partake in the joyful mystery of the Visitation. How imaginative to take such a familiar image from the pages of scripture and breathe new life into it. How familiarly Thea-esque. How Christ-like. Surely the great wing-span of the Holy Spirit hovers continuously over that house.

At the time I met them, the sisters had an image of the Visitation hanging over the fireplace in the living room. Not only was it from the Renaissance, but it was German, so we were looking at a painting of two chubby hausfraus with blonde hair and rosy cheeks embracing each other in their fifteenth-century garb. My friend Linda, seated next to me, leaned over and whispered, "What is THAT doing here?" and the next thing I knew she and her husband Joel had commissioned from me an Afro-centric rendition of this timeless mystery for the nuns in the 'hood.

I'd had Thea in me for a good year by this time, so I knew how to do black. Because of the timing of the commission and for whom it was being painted, and because of the stories and memories that now filled my heart, and mostly because I needed the work, I accepted this project with great enthusiasm. I felt surrounded by saints and ancestors as my parents, Thea, Mary, and Elizabeth, each revealed to me the deep and mysterious ways in which God visits us and we visit each other with God. St Francis DeSales said, "Lips can only speak to ears, but hearts speak to hearts." In

that spirit the Windsock Visitation was born.

On the day of the unveiling, the sisters gathered twenty excited kids from the neighborhood who sat cross-legged on the living room floor in front of the fireplace. None of us had ever been to an official unveiling before, so there was great anticipation in the air. When the moment arrived, some prayers were said as one of the sisters pulled off the African fabric which covered the painting. A kazoo was triumphantly blown and a Jesuit friend bestowed the final blessing amid the oohs and aahs of the humble assembly. Then, I told the kids about the very special visit of Mary and Elizabeth.

I told them about Mary being a scared pregnant teenager who had a most extraordinary visit from an angel one day who invited her to be the Mother of Jesus. I told them that she said YES even though she didn't fully get it and she was a bit scared about the whole thing. She's dressed in yellow because she is a woman clothed with the sun and on her cape are the star of Bethlehem and the cross of Calvary, symbols of Christ's humanity. But the story just gets better and better because Mary decided to put her own fears aside and go visit her cousin Elizabeth, who was going to have a baby named John the Baptist, even though she was way too old to be anything but somebody's great-grandmother.

I told them that we all need an Elizabeth in

our lives, someone to tell us that "it's gonna be alright, stop being afraid, God is here, so just keep on stepping." I mentioned that we get more beautiful as we get older, just like Elizabeth, because of our stories and memories and wisdom from God. That's why her halo is copper, because it ages beautifully.

I told the kids that the wind of the Holy Spirit blows through each of our life stories just like the windsock hanging in front of the sisters' house; that each of us, male or female, carries Jesus inside of us and He teaches us how to love and be loved in return. Like Mary, we must carry that love to other folks when they need it and like Elizabeth we must answer when there is a knock at the door because it just might be God doing the knocking.

When a little girl asked me why I painted gold dishes behind the women's heads, I told her that they are really symbols of the light that glows from inside each of us. We are all children of God, I said, and God has given each of us a gift, a little light. God didn't give us this light to just sit on it, we're supposed to share it, this little light.

Let it shine.

Let it shine.

Let it shine.

About the Author

Brother Mickey McGrath is an Oblate of St. Francis DeSales who lives in his hometown of Philadelphia and works out of his studio in a Catholic school. When not painting and writing, Mickey is a frequent speaker at parish retreats and conferences for Catholic teachers and catechists. No matter the topic, his theme is always the same: that art and story offer the best (and most fun) ways to evangelize and share the faith.

Mickey has been engaged in art ministry on a fulltime basis since 1994, but prior to that, he taught art and art history at DeSales University in Pennsylvania. Since 1987, he has taught classes on art and faith at the Grunewald Guild, an ecumenical art community in Leavenworth, Washington, and recently he served one year as artist-in-residence at the Washington Theological Union in Washington, DC.

Over the years, Mickey has illustrated and/or written a dozen award-winning books on Jesus, Mary, and the saints for various publishers, including *Women of Mercy* (Orbis Books, 2005).

Mickey was honored to be the recipient of the *Thea Bowman Black Catholic Education Award* at Duquesne University in 2008 for his efforts in presenting *This Little Light*, his painted stories of Thea Bowman, at over 50 venues throughout the United States.

No matter the work or venue, Mickey borrows his life motto from St. Francis DeSales, who once said, "We pray best before beauty."